10 SUPERPOWERS of Effective Leaders

Neutralizing Toxicity in Team Culture

NATALIE B. GREEN

GREEN HERITAGE
PUBLISHING

Copyright © 2023 Natalie B. Green ALL RIGHTS RESERVED.

No part of this book or its associated ancillary materials may be reproduced or transmitted in any form or by any means, electronic or mechanical, including photocopying, recording, or by any informational storage or retrieval system without permission from the publisher.

PUBLISHED BY: Green Heritage Publishing

DISCLAIMER AND/OR LEGAL NOTICES While all attempts have been made to verify information provided in this book and its ancillary materials, neither the author or publisher assumes any responsibility for errors, inaccuracies or omissions and is not responsible for any financial loss by customer in any manner. Any slights of people or organizations are unintentional. If advice concerning legal, financial, accounting, or related matters is needed, the services of a qualified professional should be sought. This book and its associated ancillary materials, including verbal and written training, is not intended for use as a source of legal, financial, or accounting advice. You should be aware of the various laws governing business transactions or other business practices in your particular geographical location.

EARNINGS & INCOME DISCLAIMER With respect to the reliability, accuracy, timeliness, usefulness, adequacy, completeness, and/ or suitability of information provided in this book, Natalie B. Green, its partners, associates, affiliates, consultants, and/or presenters make no warranties, guarantees, representations, or claims of any kind. Readers' results will vary depending on a number of factors. Any and all claims or representations as to income earnings are not to be considered as average earnings. Testimonials are not representative. This book and all products and services are for educational and informational purposes only. Use caution and see the advice of qualified professionals. Check with your accountant, attorney, or professional advisor before acting on this or any information. You agree that James Malinchak and/or Natalie B. Green is not responsible for the success or failure of your personal, business, health or financial decisions relating to any information presented by Natalie B. Green, or company products/services. Earnings potential is entirely dependent on the efforts, skills, and application of the individual person. Any examples, stories, references, or case studies are for illustrative purposes only and should not be interpreted as testimonies and/or examples of what readers and/or consumers can generally expect from the information. No representation in any part of this information, materials and/or seminar training are guarantees or promises for actual performance. Any statements, strategies, concepts, techniques, exercises and ideas in the information, materials and/or seminar training offered are simply opinion or experience, and thus should not be misinterpreted as promises, typical results or guarantees (expressed or implied). The author and publisher (Natalie B. Green or any of Natalie B. Green's representatives) shall in no way, under any circumstances, be held liable to any party (or third party) for any direct, indirect, punitive, special, incidental, or other consequential damages arising directly or indirectly from any use of books, materials and or seminar trainings, which is provided "as is," and without warranties.

10 Superpowers of Effective Leaders – Neutralizing Toxicity in Team Culture

ISBN: 978-0-9600299-2-1

For Worldwide Distribution, Printed in the U.S.A.

Cover Design by Trey Simon

Photography by Created-N-Love Studios

www.nataliebgreen.com

What people are saying about Natalie B. Green and her strategies

"I loved this book. It was to the point: Simple, but not simplified; powerful, but not heavy handed. This is hard to quantify, but while reading the great insights contained in this work, I felt like I was being given loving advice and input from a friend who cared about helping make me successful.

The practical implementation strategies at the end of each chapter make the superpowers accessible and attainable. Anyone who reads and applies the wisdom shared here will undoubtedly improve both themselves and the team they lead."

                                    -Jason Perry, Director
                                          Oak Tree Leadership

"Have you wondered if your style of leadership is contributing to a toxic culture in the work, organization, or your home environment? Why do some leaders seem to be better equipped to lead than others? In 10 Superpowers of Effective Leaders, Natalie B. Green helps the reader to understand that leadership is not based on the title that you wear but is an inherent quality that can be found in anyone.

Therefore, it is important that leaders possess character traits that promote an atmosphere that is conducive to building individuals, and team members all the while evaluating and confronting their own strengths and weaknesses. However, Natalie doesn't stop there, this book lays out very clearly and concisely what makes for a toxic culture and how to overcome toxicity in your leadership style and in the culture that you are leading. Get ready to go to another level of leadership with the 10 Superpowers of Effective Leaders."

-**Dr. Joann M. John**, President/CEO
Academy of Biblical Training, Inc.

"In the same manner that makes music a universal language ... "The power of a team lies in its diversity, and effective leaders understand that embracing and supporting differences can lead to greater success than conformity to sameness ever could" is a universal truth. Leaders who embrace this truth will not only neutralize toxicity in their teams but they themselves will become more effective and relatable leaders.

Humans have five senses: vision, hearing, touch, smell, and taste. All of these senses are important in our daily lives. In reading **10 Superpowers of Effective Leaders**, it's as if I gained a sixth sense; a greater knowing of who I am from who I was and where I came from and where I'm headed. I highly recommend this book for leaders and aspiring leaders – it's an eye and soul opener.

It's true that leaders are not born with superpowers but

what we learn, live and experience in life is what uniquely sets us apart. Leading from those unique spaces in truth, authenticity and empathy makes one an effective leader. Because of "10 Superpowers of Effective Leaders" somewhere in the future you look much better than you do right now.

Thanks, Natalie, for bringing this transformative gem to us in a super powerful read."

-**Nouchelle Hastings,** Managing Partner
Relevant Book Publishing Company

"This book is a must have for every leadership type! "The Superpowers of Effective Leaders" is brilliantly constructed by the author. It contains thought provoking quotes, inspiring insights, and a plan of action to help integrate what you've learned. I love the literary style of this book. It's an easy read, but acts as a training guide, giving you not only the diagnosis but also the prescription.

It is the prevention but also the cure for a healthy team dynamic. Natalie equips you with the what, the why and the how in such a concise and relatable way that it is impossible not to be transformed. For every leader who wants to leverage their impact, influence, and income, I highly recommend this book!"

-**Dr. Samantha Williams,** Pastor
Author | Leadership Coach

"10 Superpowers of Effective Leaders: *Neutralizing Toxicity in Team Culture* by Natalie B. Green is a great book on effective leadership, and in it, the author answers the question: What does it take for leaders to lead successfully absent of toxic baggage? Presenting a work that involves in-depth research and personal encounters, the author identifies key qualities of effective leaders and highlight some of the things that change the game in leadership, including effective communication, collaboration, taking ownership, self-awareness, and more. While the book provides a proven path to successful leadership, it features 10 chapters that are educative and self-checks at the same time. Readers learn from a seasoned leader and define their leadership style through the well-thought-out simple steps presents.

The writing itself is beautiful and ordinary readers will find it easy to access the information that is so generously shared. This book is a gem for aspiring leaders and anyone who wants to lead better; it redefines the key tenets of leadership and provides tools that will help readers take control of their journey towards effectively leading others. Natalie B. Green understands what readers need and she delivers it with style and flair, communicating what is essential in a language that is beautiful and with authority that grabs readers by the hand and leads them toward their leadership goals."

-**Dr. Erania J. Witherspoon**, Founder
Soul-Lifted Sisters Outreach Organization

"10 Superpowers of Effective Leaders by Natalie B. Green is a must have! It is a book that empowers aspiring, emerging, and mature leaders to use and develop the skills and gifts they have, to achieve team goals. While this book may appear to be a short read, it is insightful, penned simplistically and practically to help you as a leader understand the SUPERPOWER you must possess. Every chapter has a way of building you up and making you aware of the greatness you already possess inside. However, this book challenges you to reflect and look introspectively because you may have some tweaking to do to ensure you don't compete with others, instead you compliment them.

I love the tone in which Natalie writes. It's very inviting, soft spoken, yet real and honest. You can feel her heart as I'm sure she's experienced things while being a part of a team, so the wisdom she pours into this book is valid and true. I love how she gives reflection or action steps at the end. It reminds the reader of what they just read and the author highlights what's really important."

Char-Michelle McDowell
Author | Entrepreneur | Speaker
Just B.E.E. IT! – A guide to finding your fit and living with bold

INSPIRE OTHER TO LEAD WELL!

Share This Book

Retail $21.99

Special Quantity (Paperback)

5-20 Books	$19.99
21-99 Books	$17.99
100-499 Books	$15.99
500-999 Books	$13.99
1000+ Books	$10.99

To Place an Order Contact:

www.nataliebgreen.com
natalie@nataliebgreen.com
(305) 205-6820

> We were all born with a certain degree of power. The key to success is discovering this innate power and using it daily to deal with whatever challenges come our way.
>
> -Les Brown

THE IDEAL PROFESSIONAL SPEAKER FOR YOUR NEXT EVENT!

Any organization that wants to develop their people to become "extraordinary," needs to hire Natalie B. Green for a keynote and/or workshop training!

TO CONTACT OR BOOK
Natalie B. Green

TO SPEAK:

www.nataliebgreen.com
natalie@nataliebgreen.com
(305) 205-6820

"Leaders who lack awareness of their own assets and deficits are likely to misjudge the strengths and weaknesses of their team members."

THE IDEAL COACH FOR YOU!

If you're ready to overcome challenges, have major breakthroughs and achieve higher levels, then you will love having Natalie B. Green as your coach!

TO CONTACT
Natalie B. Green

FOR COACHING:

www.nataliebgreen.com
natalie@nataliebgreen.com
(305) 205-6820

"Everything rises and falls on leadership."

-John C. Maxwell

Dedication

This book's dedication begins with heartfelt appreciation for my well-loved late mother, Mandy J. Jones (Biscuit), who demonstrated in life what it means to be committed to the success of the entire team, which was her family. Her invaluable life lessons continue to shine as a guiding beacon, igniting the flames of passion and purpose within the individuals I have the privilege to lead.

Additionally, I extend my dedication to those who have graciously allowed me to learn and grow as a leader. I am deeply thankful for the privilege of refining my leadership abilities, a journey made possible by your gracious-ness, patience, and unwavering belief in the person I aspire to become.

To my immediate family and the congregation of my church, your unwavering faith and support have been a constant source of strength as I navigate the path toward fully embracing my true identity. I am forever grateful!

> "Expect the best. Prepare for the worst. Capitalize on what comes."
>
> -Zig Ziglar

Table of Contents

A Message To You 1
Superpower 1: Born to Lead 5
Superpower 2: Self-Awareness 11
Superpower 3: The Non-Compete 15
Superpower 4: Value Added 21
Superpower 5: Empower 26
Superpower 6: Silence 30
Superpower 7: Listen With Your Ears 35
Superpower 8: Open Minds 41
Superpower 9: Leverage Time 45
Superpower 10: Dirty Hands 51
Conclusion 56
About the Author 58
Affirmations for Superpowered Leader 61
Contact 61

"Effective leaders are acutely aware of the advantages that come with rolling up their sleeves."

A Message To You

With over four decades of experience navigating a multitude of toxic environments, I stand before you as someone who believes in teaching individuals to fish, equipping them with the skills to sustain themselves for a lifetime. It is my unwavering conviction that I've been entrusted with a mission—to empower others to thrive in work, service, play, and life within an environment that harmoniously accommodates their differences.

In a world that often clamors for conformity, we frequently find ourselves challenged to suppress our unique qualities. Yet, it is precisely in the celebration and acceptance of these differences that we unlock the boundless potential for creativity and progress within teams and organizations. Effective leaders recognize this profound truth, possessing the ability to harness the diverse talents of their team members, thereby elevating productivity and deftly neutralizing the toxicity that may lurk among their ranks. This journey toward effective leadership, while preserving the individual nuances that make each person unique, forms the cornerstone of the ten superpowers explored within the pages of this book.

10 Superpowers of Effective Leaders

10 Superpowers of Effective Leaders: Neutralizing Toxicity in Team Culture is for anyone who finds themselves in a stressful, overwhelming, taxing, and toxic work, team, social, or religious setting. Whether you are a leader or an emerging leader, the superpowers discussed in this book can serve as a launch pad for adding a great deal of value to your team and assist you in creating a culture of success- free from toxicity. While this list of superpowers is not exhaustive, it is intentional and purposeful in helping leaders identify and cultivate skills that can be an enduring benefit to the entire team.

The goal is to foster an environment where individuals and teams can work together in harmony toward a common goal without being weighed down by stress and toxicity. This requires intentionality, investment in the good of the team, and a refusal to adapt to toxic cultures that have become normalized. The power of a team lies in its diversity, and effective leaders understand that embracing and supporting differences can lead to greater success than conformity to sameness ever could.

By adopting the concepts outlined in this book, leaders can learn to effectively harness the unique skills, strengths, and abilities of their team members, which will increase productivity and reduce stress. The key is to create a culture that is innovative, productive, and supportive of individual differences. This will require leaders to be intentional and invest in their team members' growth, individually and collectively.

A Message to You

In conclusion, by embracing and supporting differences among team members, leaders can neutralize toxic cultures and create an environment that adds value to everyone involved. The journey towards effective leadership is a continuous one, and this book serves as a starting point for those who want to develop the skills and abilities necessary to lead their team to success, absent of toxic baggage.

Take a Moment

Before you get started on this journey, make a list of what you expect to gain from 10 Superpowers of Effective Leaders.

_____

_____

_____

_____

_____

_____

_____

_____

_____

_____

_____

_____

SUPERPOWER 1

Born to Lead

At the outset, I want to dispel the notion that being a leader is reserved for only those with fancy titles and a domineering demeanor. In my view, leadership is a quality that can be found in anyone. The traditional image of a leader as someone who barks orders and demands compliance is more akin to a tyrant than a true leader.

The greatest leader ever is the one who leads himself well.

I love the simple definition of a leader that I heard from John Maxwell, a renowned leadership expert. He said in an interview that "a leader is a person who influences others." This means that anyone who can sway people towards a particular idea or action can be considered a leader, whether it be a parent, boss, supervisor, or co-worker. You could say you were born to lead.

We have learned to think so differently about what a

leader looks like that we have overlooked and even dismissed our personal position as a leader. I believe that leadership is innate and that every person is born with the potential to be a leader. Can you remember the admonishments of your parents as a youngster to be a leader, not a follower? Those wise words were spoken to keep you in line but could have been some of the best advice you've ever received.

Realizing that you have the born leader superpower can give you a sense of confidence and purpose in life, business, and service to others. The primary position of a leader is in the forefront, where others watch and learn. Leaders must be aware that there are impressionable people behind them looking for guidance. This awareness should instill a sense of responsibility in leaders to act in a responsible and ethical manner.

Individuals often contemplate the purpose of their existence and life's ultimate goal. I believe that we are all born to lead in our own way, but many fail to recognize this superpower. Once we become aware of our leadership potential, toxic behaviors such as the need to be the center of attention or the expert on everything will no longer be a necessary coping mechanism.

As a result, toxicity within us will not spill over onto our teams because we know who we are and what we bring to the table. The greatest leader ever is the one who leads himself well. By leading ourselves well, we can create a positive impact on those around us.

By following these steps, you can not only recognize your innate leadership potential but also harness it to become a more authentic and effective leader, both in your personal and professional life:

1. **Recognize the Inclusivity of Leadership:**

   - Understand that leadership is not confined to individuals with prestigious titles or dominant personalities.
   - Embrace the idea that leadership is a quality inherent in anyone who can influence others' thoughts or actions, whether in the roles of a parent, boss, or supervisor.
   - Internalize John Maxwell's definition of a leader as someone who influences others and realize that this definition encompasses a wide range of roles and responsibilities.

2. **Discover Your Unique Leadership Style:**

   - Reflect on your personal journey and experiences to uncover your distinct leadership qualities.
   - Understand that your leadership style may differ from traditional expectations, and that's perfectly acceptable.
   - Embrace your individuality as a leader, recognizing that your unique perspective and approach can be your greatest strength.

3. Lead Yourself Well:

- Acknowledge the importance of self-leadership as the foundation for effective leadership of others.
- Cultivate self-awareness and self-acceptance to avoid fueling toxicity within yourself.
- Focus on understanding and embracing your natural strengths, which will empower you to lead authentically and create a positive impact on those around you.

I remember a time in my own journey when I was finding my footing as a leader and a speaker. I would get invitations to speak but left most engagements in a bit of amazement. I struggled with understanding why people reacted the way they did to what I had to say. Why were so many moved and impacted by my simple words? I was far from eloquent and probably spoke with a touch of "hood." What I shared as a speaker came so naturally to me that I missed the value of it.

Despite my imperfect delivery, I found that people were still moved by my words. It took some time to realize that I was fueling toxicity within myself by not recognizing the value of my own unique perspective. There was a day when I simply accepted my style and my story as my strength. Suddenly, the light came on, and I realized that I was not struggling to find my voice; my struggle was recognizing the value of what I had to say. I was fueling toxicity within myself, which could easily have affected everyone around me.

Once I embraced what came naturally, I realized what I was born for. I was not meant to sound like, look like, or be like anyone else. I had to learn to embrace the person I was born to be. I finally understood that I was involved in or doing too many things that did not enhance my leadership skills or abilities, which led me away from the person I was born to be – a leader in my own right. I felt inadequate because my leadership looked different than someone else's did. It's important to remember that sameness is not always desirable or necessary in effective leadership and that it is our difference that makes us unique and is also what gives us our highest value.

Take a Moment

Use this space to make a list of ways you intend to redefine what a true leader looks like.

_____

_____

_____

_____

_____

_____

_____

_____

_____

_____

SUPERPOWER 2

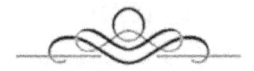

Self-Awareness

In my role as an entrepreneur, minister, and coach, I have had the opportunity to interact with people from various backgrounds, including those who are in what is considered leadership positions. Being someone who enjoys problem-solving and studying human behavior, I take the time to listen carefully to people and pay attention to the unspoken aspects of their communication. Often, people approach me when they face obstacles or challenges in their business, team, or leadership role. After they share their concerns with me, I ask them to reflect on how they got to this point. Interestingly, very few people admit to being the cause of the problem.

Leaders who lack awareness of their own assets and deficits are likely to misjudge the strengths and weaknesses of their team members.

The New Oxford American Dictionary defines self-awareness as *conscious knowledge of one's own character, feelings,* *motives, and desires.*

The superpower of self-awareness is crucial for any successful leader. When leaders are self-aware and acknowledge how their strengths and weaknesses impact their leadership style, they set themselves up for success. Leaders who lack awareness of their own assets and deficits are likely to misjudge the strengths and weaknesses of their team members. In contrast, leaders who possess self-awareness tend to be more empathetic, compassionate, and relatable to their team. They understand that everyone has areas of strength and weakness and assign tasks accordingly. By doing so, they increase the team's motivation and reduce the likelihood of toxic team dynamics.

Self-aware leaders are also better equipped to identify and address their own weaknesses and those of their team members. They achieve this through structured training, workshops, and collaborations. By acknowledging their limitations and working to improve upon them, effective leaders foster growth and development within their teams. Admitting to one's weaknesses can be challenging, especially for those in leadership positions. However, ignoring one's shortcomings only leads to stagnation and toxicity within the team. Being open and honest about one's weaknesses helps to build a dream team that complements each other's strengths and makes up for each other's deficits.

By following these simple steps, leaders can promote self-awareness, improve their leadership effectiveness, and build a cohesive team that works together to overcome challenges and achieve success, ultimately reducing the likelihood of toxicity within the team.

1. Reflect on Personal Strengths and Weaknesses:

- Take the time to assess your own character, feelings, motives, and desires, as defined by self-awareness.
- Reflect on how your strengths and weaknesses impact your leadership style and interactions with team members.
- Recognize that self-awareness is a crucial superpower for successful leadership, as it allows you to better understand yourself and your leadership approach.

2. Identify and Address Weaknesses:

- Actively identify your own weaknesses as a leader and be open to feedback from team members.
- Invest in structured training, workshops, or collaborations to address your limitations and enhance your leadership skills.
- Encourage team members to do the same, fostering a culture of growth and development within the team.

3. Embrace Openness and Honesty:

- Overcome the challenge of not admitting weaknesses, recognizing that it's a crucial step toward personal and team growth.
- Create an environment where team members feel comfortable discussing their own shortcomings and challenges.
- Build a diverse and complementary team where members can support each other, making up for each other's deficits and fostering a collaborative spirit.

SUPERPOWER 3

The Non-Compete

The desire to compete is deeply engrained into the fabric of human design. We all crave the "W" in some form or another; after all, who wants to be labeled a loser? Healthy competition has its place in sports and entertainment and sometimes shows up as inter-team challenges. However, when team members find themselves in competition with each other, it creates a highly toxic culture that hinders their ability to succeed.

Effective leaders do not compete with their team, instead, they leverage their skills to complete the mission, and secure a win for the team.

An effective leader should never see themselves in competition with those they lead. A competitive spirit often shows up when a team member may possess a particular quality that the leader does not. To compensate, the leader may posture themselves competitively against their own team member in hopes of being recognized as the star player when the goal should be to have a star team.

A leader with the non-compete superpower recognizes that no one person has all the necessary qualities for success and that every team member is essential to achieving the team's goals. They understand that it is the coming together of all the moving parts that make the machine run smoothly and effectively. Every part has its place and is intrinsically vital to the performance of the team's mission.

I remember when my hometown baseball team won its first World Series. Our town was electric with excitement because our team won the biggest game in the league. As an event planner, I had the privilege of having a catcher for that team as a client. One thing that stood out at his events is that members of the team who did not bring to the game the same thing he did were invited to the party just the same. I acquired other clients from the team, which gave me insight into the camaraderie between the players, which was a crucial factor in the team's ability to bring home the win and the ring.

A leader who desires to be effective should avoid competing with team members by celebrating their unique talents and strengths. It is quite difficult to publicly celebrate a team member's attributes while secretly competing with them or trying to prevent them from using their talents for the good of the team. A leader who embraces their own qualities and encourages their team members to do the same will create a positive and collaborative environment. Using this non-compete superpower will eliminate the team's urge to embrace a toxic competitive model.

Here are three steps to help you steer clear of the pitfall of competing with those you're leading while preparing your team for goal achievement and project completion within a cooperative and harmonious team environment:

1. Acknowledge and Celebrate Individual Strengths:

- Recognize that every team member possesses unique talents and qualities that contribute to the team's success.
- Identify and celebrate these individual strengths openly and genuinely.
- Encourage team members to embrace and showcase their strengths, fostering a collaborative environment where everyone's contributions are valued.

2. Promote a Unified Team Vision:

- Shift the focus from individual competition to a collective team vision.
- Emphasize that the team's goal is to work together and achieve success as a unified group.
- Encourage team members to see themselves as

essential parts of a well-oiled machine, with each person playing a crucial role in the team's overall performance.

3. Lead by Example:

- Demonstrate the non-compete superpower by showcasing your confidence in your own qualities and abilities.
- Avoid any hidden competitive behaviors or attempts to undermine team members' contributions.
- Create an environment where open collaboration and mutual support are encouraged, demonstrating that everyone can achieve more significant victories when working together toward a common goal.

By following these steps, you can lead with a non-competitive mindset, celebrating individual strengths, fostering a sense of unity, and promoting a team-focused approach to success, ultimately reducing toxicity within the team, and achieving more significant victories together. Remember, a competition's goal is to prove that one is better than the other. However, if the focus shifts from "you vs. me" to "us" or "we," everyone can benefit from each other's contributions. Ultimately, a leader's goal should be to create a winning environment for everyone. Competition may breed success in some areas, but a team that works together towards a common goal will ultimately achieve more significant victories.

> *"People who add value to others do so intentionally."*
> —John C. Maxwell

SUPERPOWER 4

Value Added

In today's world, the definition of a leader has been distorted by old-fashioned paradigms, causing us to believe that leaders only make demands without adding anything to the team. In this chapter, we need to reconsider the expectations of leaders and followers. Based on the idea that a leader is a person who influences others, we can imagine that leaders are not just those who subtract from the team but also those who add to it. Effective leaders increase their influence by intentionally adding value to people.

Effective leaders increase their influence by intentionally adding value to people.

Adding value to the team is a crucial superpower for a leader to possess if they desire to increase their influence in their team's life. It may be difficult to think of ways to add value besides giving directives or assignments. Leaders who take the time to really see their team members avail themselves of the unique opportunity of identifying areas of need within them. Armed with this evaluation, the effective leader can be intentional about helping team members to become a greater asset to the team. Whether it's personal or professional growth, when all the links in the chain are strong, the chances of getting the job done well are inevitable. It is important to understand that adding value to a person goes beyond a paycheck; it creates something extraordinary for both the leader and the recipient.

I think that leaders who embrace the role of adding value experience a heightened sense of purpose and achievement. Over the years, I have deliberately focused on "being" added value to individuals in and outside of the workplace. I recognize that this approach significantly contributes to my effectiveness as a leader across different fields of interest.

Effective leaders adopt adding value to others as second nature, especially in a results-driven world. When a leader adds value to their team, their loyalty and commitment to the cause becomes unquestionable. Each member of your team has the potential to be an asset and not a liability. Sometimes, the least likely to succeed on a team can become the top performer if only someone took the time to help them fortify their areas of weakness. Your team's weakest link could be the perfect match, but adding value to them can make all the difference. Adding value to team members is essential for individual success as well as the overall success of the team.

Value Added

Recognizing team members for their contributions to the team is crucial in making them feel valued. Leaders should also be sensitive to personal situations and make adjustments to accommodate special needs. Adding value looks different depending on the need, but leaders who are determined to add value will always find a way to do so.

It is necessary for leaders to evaluate themselves regularly and determine if their interactions with their team added value or subtracted value from it. This does not mean avoiding adverse situations or neglecting areas of concern in a project.

By implementing the following strategies, leaders can effectively add value to their team members, creating an environment of growth, loyalty, and commitment, ultimately contributing to the team's overall success:

1. Identify Individual Needs and Growth Opportunities:

- Take the time to truly understand each team member's strengths, weaknesses, and areas of need.
- Provide personalized support and guidance to help team members grow personally and professionally.
- Recognize that strong, well-developed individuals contribute to a more successful team.

2. Foster a Sense of Purpose and Achievement:

- Encourage team members to see their work as meaningful and purposeful within the team's mission.
- Highlight the value each team member brings to the collective effort, reinforcing their sense of achievement.
- Show that their contributions go beyond a paycheck, creating a sense of fulfillment for both the leader and the team member.

3. Promote Loyalty and Commitment:

- Build strong, loyal relationships with your team members by consistently adding value to their lives.
- When team members feel valued and supported, their loyalty to the team and commitment to its goals become unwavering.
- Recognize that every team member has the potential to be an asset and help them unlock their hidden potential.

4. Recognize and Accommodate Individual Needs:

- Acknowledge team members for their contributions and make them feel valued for their unique strengths.
- Be sensitive to personal situations and make accommodation when necessary to support team

members' well-being.
- Understand that adding value can take different forms depending on individual needs.

5. Evaluate and Self-Reflect Regularly:

- Continuously assess your interactions with the team to determine whether they add or subtract value.
- Embrace difficult situations and address areas of concern within projects or team dynamics without neglecting them.
- Make adding value a habitual practice to foster a culture of value within the team, leading to growth, harmony, and success.

In conclusion, leaders must recognize their superpower of adding value to their team members. Leaders who add value to their team increase their influence, loyalty, and commitment to the cause, ultimately leading to the success of the team. By making adding value a habit, leaders create a culture of value that minimizes pushback, encourages growth, and fosters a supportive and harmonious environment.

SUPERPOWER 5

Empower

In the preceding chapter, we delved into the concept of the superpower that is added value. It's important to recognize that the act of adding value and the practice of empowering team members are deeply intertwined. Earlier, we touched upon the age-old analogy of teaching someone to fish, a reflection of my natural inclination toward empowering those within my sphere of influence. In my role as a coach, I am granted a unique vantage point to witness the profound impact of empowering my clients to achieve success from within themselves, a stark departure from simply handing them a checklist of tasks to accomplish a specific goal.

Empowering people sets them up for future success.

Empowering an individual is akin to illuminating the metaphorical lightbulb within them. As leaders, we often establish systems and protocols as the primary means by which tasks or projects should be executed. Undoubtedly, these systems can lead to success when they are designed for broad applicability. However, I firmly believe that a higher degree of success is attainable when team members internalize the methodology, possessing an intuitive understanding of it. We refer to this as knowing it by heart. When an individual not only comprehends the destination and route but also carries it within them, they gain the ability to adapt when confronted with roadblocks.

It is vital to grasp that empowering your team extends beyond the provision of systems and protocols. It necessitates granting them the requisite authority to draw upon their own skill sets and practical experiences within the framework of their expertise. I reminisce about a past role in a fast-paced work environment rife with numerous concurrent activities. To ensure optimal functionality, I had to devise a system aligned with existing protocols to meet the demands of the job. However, I also needed the authority to make real-time adjustments, as unexpected challenges frequently arose.

We have explored the symbiotic relationship between adding value and empowering team members, emphasizing the importance of kindling the light of empowerment within individuals. In the previous paragraph, I used the term "authority." We empower our team members when we entrust them with the authority to employ their strengths, skills, and knowledge effectively. Failing to grant some latitude in this regard may inadvertently stifle their potential for future success. Leaders must recognize that their willingness to relinquish some control can be the catalyst for unlocking their team's full potential and driving future success.

Through the following four strategies, leaders can empower their team members, reduce toxic control, and foster a more collaborative and adaptive work environment, ultimately setting the stage for future success:

1. Internalize Methodology and Foster Adaptability:

- Encourage team members to go beyond following rigid systems and protocols.
- Empower them to internalize the methodology and develop an intuitive understanding of the processes.
- This approach allows team members to adapt and find creative solutions when faced with challenges, reducing frustration and toxicity.

2. Grant Authority and Autonomy:

- Provide team members with the authority to leverage their unique skills, strengths, and practical experiences.
- Allow them to make real-time decisions and adjustments within the framework of their expertise.
- Empowering team members with autonomy boosts their confidence and ownership, reducing the need for micromanagement and toxic

control.

3. Kindle the Light of Empowerment:

- Recognize that empowering team members goes beyond implementing systems and protocols.
- Focus on igniting the metaphorical lightbulb within them, helping them understand and embrace their roles.
- Encourage team members to take ownership of their tasks and responsibilities, fostering a sense of purpose and initiative.

4. Relinquish Control and Unlock Potential:

- Understand that leaders must be willing to relinquish some control to unlock the team's full potential.
- Empowerment requires trusting your team to use their strengths and expertise effectively.
- By doing so, leaders create a collaborative and supportive environment that reduces toxicity, as team members feel valued, trusted, and motivated to contribute their best.

SUPERPOWER 6

Silence

For individuals who are not quite comfortable with their identity as a leader, taking charge can be a challenging task. Such leaders may lack confidence in their position of authority or struggle to recognize their value to the team. These insecurities may lead them to overcompensate by talking excessively, inadvertently exposing their weaknesses.

A great quality of an effective leader is the ability to read the room, which sometimes requires the leader to be quiet.

Leadership isn't always about being the loudest voice in the room; sometimes, it's about the strength of silence. In their attempt to seek validation, leaders with low self-confidence may resort to being the loudest voice in the room. However, this behavior can hinder their growth and even sabotage their future advancement. It can also undermine the team's confidence in their leadership as they fail to discern the appropriate moment to speak.

In contrast, leaders who possess the superpower of

silence gain valuable insights into their team's mindset, productivity methodologies, and dynamics that impact performance. By observing quietly, they can make significant contributions to achieving the team's objectives. Through silence, they can assess each team member's capabilities, identifying those who possess unique qualities to add value to the effort.

Silence has several benefits, one of which is that it allows team members to voice their opinions without fear of judgment. This promotes participation and fosters a sense of ownership and commitment to the mission's success. Silence is often seen as a virtue indicative of wisdom and depth, and leaders who are comfortable with silence command attention when they decide to speak.

Leaders who talk excessively are not effective and rarely capture the audience's interest. In contrast, those who use their words sparingly and thoughtfully have a greater impact due to the perspective gained through silent observation. By doing so, they leave no room for confusion, defusing any tendencies toward toxicity due to conjecture.

Effective communication involves both verbal and non-verbal techniques. The adage "still waters run deep" rings true when it comes to harnessing the benefits of silence in the team setting. A leader who commands the audience's attention when they speak should ensure that their words are few, on topic, and timed precisely for maximum impact. By asking their team members for input and acknowledging their contributions, leaders can put out any fires of toxicity that may be brewing.

These three steps will help you on your quiet strength journey:

1. Enhance Self-Confidence and Empower the Team:

- Understand that effective leadership doesn't always require speaking the loudest or most frequently.
- Embrace the superpower of silence to gain insights into your team's dynamics, productivity, and individual strengths.
- Encourage team members to voice their opinions without fear of judgment, creating a more inclusive and open communication environment that reduces toxicity.

2. Maximize Impactful Communication:

- Realize that leaders who talk excessively can often dilute their messages and lose their audience's interest.
- Use words thoughtfully and sparingly, ensuring that when you do speak, your words carry weight and clarity.
- Acknowledge the power of silence in providing you with perspective and depth that can enhance your verbal communication.

- Lead by example, demonstrating the value of listening and measured speech to your team, which can encourage healthier communication patterns and reduce misunderstandings.

3. Learn from Others and Foster Humility:

- Recognize that effective leadership involves continuous learning, even from team members, subordinates, or superiors.
- Embrace the practice of communicating through silence when you're in the company of experienced leaders, as it can be a humbling and educational experience.
- By actively listening and observing during moments of silence, you can gain valuable insights and learn from the wisdom of others.
- This approach not only enriches your leadership skills but also reduces toxicity by promoting a culture of respect and open learning within the team.

A great quality of an effective leader is the ability to read the room, which sometimes requires the leader to be quiet. Effective leaders know that when they are in a room of experienced leaders, it is crucial to communicate through silence and learn from them, whether they are subordinates or superiors. This approach to leadership can be humbling, and I am looking forward to exploring it further in the coming chapters.

Take a Moment

You've come a long way! Take a moment to reflect and list key principles you will use to become a more effective leader.

_____

_____

_____

_____

_____

_____

_____

_____

_____

_____

_____

SUPERPOWER 7

Listen With Your Ears

If I had to produce a top 5 list of must-have attributes of effective leaders, the superpower of listening with your ears would be among the top 3. In this post-pandemic age in which we are living, workplace toxicity, along with mental and emotional pressure, is a matter of fact. Many people are opting out of working in traditional settings and preferring to work remotely. Employees are choosing to park themselves in a space where minimal interaction is required and the potential for negative confrontations is less likely to take place.

Listening with your ears is a learned but essential behavior.

Having spent much time in working environments where some of the leaders lacked the problem-solving skill necessary to conflicts in a manner that left all parties involved feeling heard, I completely understand the thinking of many who choose to participate in isolation. When a leader possesses the superpower of listening with their ears, problems can be resolved in a more amicable manner while leaving team members' dignity intact. The concept of listening with your ears serves well in many aspects of life and relationships.

When a person finds themselves in any kind of conversation, they want to be heard. This need to be heard intensifies when the conversation is regarding some form of conflict or disagreement. The last thing the leader wants to do when attempting to deal with conflict between members of a team is to not give full attention to the members while they are sharing their concerns. When addressing team conflicts, leaders must avoid the temptation to interject with their own opinions and instead focus on active listening.

I know that I have been guilty of only listening for an opening to give my two cents and not really engaging in what the other person was saying. I was listening with my mouth. Effective leaders must understand the importance of listening with their ears and not with their mouth. A better approach for leaders dealing with team members, whether in conflict or not, includes:

1. Practice Active Listening:

- Make a conscious effort to actively listen to team members when they speak.
- Avoid interrupting or formulating responses while they are sharing their thoughts.
- Letting them know you're taking notes to capture their thoughts accurately.

Listen With Your Ears

- Show that you are fully engaged by maintaining eye contact and offering verbal cues like nodding or "I see."

2. Demonstrate Empathy and Understanding:

- Let team members know that you understand their perspective and feelings.
- Acknowledge their emotions and validate their concerns, even in times of conflict.
- This empathetic approach helps team members feel heard and valued.

3. Engage in Two-Way Communication:

- Create an open and inclusive dialogue where team members feel comfortable expressing themselves.
- Encourage all parties involved in a discussion or conflict to share their viewpoints.
- Foster an environment where constructive feedback and diverse opinions are welcomed.

4. Summarize and Reflect:

- After team members have spoken, summarize the key points you've heard from each person.
- Reflect on their perspectives and concerns to ensure you have grasped their viewpoints accurately.
- This practice demonstrates your commitment to

understanding their positions.

5. Avoid Preemptive Solutions:

- Resist the urge to jump in with your own opinions or solutions during discussions.
- Focus on active listening and seeking clarity before offering your input.
- By refraining from premature judgments, you create space for collaborative problem-solving and conflict resolution.

By implementing these approaches, leaders can enhance their listening skills, foster open communication, and reduce the potential for workplace toxicity. This, in turn, strengthens team cohesion and promotes a more harmonious and productive work environment.

Once team members are aware that the leader is listening with intention to gain clarity on the situation, they will be open to constructive criticism as well as advice on a reasonable solution to the problem at hand. Listening with your ears is a learned but essential behavior, especially if you are already aware of the cause of the problem as well as the solution. However, it's crucial to remember that as a leader, you should always strive to add value to those you lead.

Listening with an open mind can also provide valuable insights, as frontline team members often possess unique perspectives due to their proximity to the task at hand. If your team members believe that you don't hear them, they will not be willing to wholeheartedly invest themselves in the success of the overall effort.

True leadership is an attitude that naturally inspires and motivates others, and it comes from an internalized discovery about yourself.

-Dr. Myles Munroe

SUPERPOWER 8

Open Minds

Becoming ensnared in a single approach to achieving success can spell disaster for an otherwise thriving endeavor. An effective leader who embraces the superpower of open-mindedness positions themselves for long-term success in a constantly evolving landscape. The rise of technology has become a powerful tool, eliminating previous limitations on what could be accomplished.

Many roads lead to success, which is always the ultimate goal.

In the era of information, innovation and creativity are invaluable assets to team efforts. Tasks that once demanded hours of learning and implementation can now be mastered in mere minutes, thanks to a swift internet search or instructional videos. In this fast-paced society, effective leaders must remain receptive to fresh avenues of learning and task execution as long as they align with the primary objectives.

Effective leadership recognizes the immense value of open-mindedness, as it removes barriers to innovation and achieving what might have seemed impossible before. Embracing the open-minded approach can greatly benefit a leader's ability to identify team members' strengths and empower them to excel, surpassing predetermined project goals. Conversely, a leader who insists on rigid control risks stifling the team's efforts and fostering a disgruntled environment.

The television show *Undercover Boss* provides a compelling example of leaders with the open-minded superpower. While watching episodes of this show, I observed how some of the bosses were made aware of outdated or obsolete systems. Typically, these bosses would revamp their procedures and protocols to achieve higher levels of success, often involving the employees who identified the issues in the transition process.

Change is rarely easy to accept, but it is an inevitable aspect of life. A leader who clings to outdated ways of thinking and doing things is destined for stagnation and potential failure. People desire recognition and purpose, and those who feel stifled may seek new opportunities in more forward-thinking environments. Effective leaders understand that many roads lead to success, which is the ultimate goal of any undertaking.

Here are some suggestions to help you embrace the open-minded superpower:

1. Embrace Change and Innovation:

- Actively seek out and welcome new ideas, technologies, and approaches to problem-solving.
- Encourage your team to propose and experiment with innovative solutions.
- Foster a culture of continuous improvement where change is viewed as an opportunity for growth rather than a threat.

2. Active Listening and Empathy:

- Make a genuine effort to listen to your team members, acknowledging their perspectives and concerns.
- Empathize with their experiences and emotions, creating an environment where they feel heard and valued.
- Practice empathetic leadership by understanding the unique needs and strengths of each team member.

3. Open Communication and Collaboration:

- Promote open and transparent communication within your team.
- Create channels for team members to express their ideas, feedback, and concerns without fear of reprisal.
- Encourage collaboration and diversity of thought by involving team members in decision-making processes and valuing their contributions.

Approaching life, business, or ministry with a closed mind can have detrimental effects on both leadership and team members. In today's interconnected world, where opportunities abound, individuals can be left behind if they are unwilling to embrace new ideas and possibilities. Social media platforms are filled with stories of people who achieved remarkable success by venturing into uncharted territory, demonstrating that what they had to offer was in demand and valued by others who were eager to invest in it.

SUPERPOWER 9

Leverage Time

Time is an intangible force, elusive and beyond our grasp. It flows relentlessly, indifferent to our desires or control. The phrases we use, such as "wasting time" or "running out of time," may make it seem as though we hold sway over time's passage, but time marches forward, regardless of anyone's wishes.

In the realm of leadership, effective leaders understand the importance of strategic time management. The late Dr. Myles Munroe aptly described time as the "currency of life." This analogy draws a compelling parallel between time and currency, emphasizing that, like money in our pockets, time is a valuable resource for exchange.

> *Like money in our pockets, time is a valuable resource for exchange.*

Every moment spent on one activity is a moment forfeited for another. Leaders, therefore, must master the superpower of leveraging time to their advantage. While we cannot halt or expand time, we can certainly make astute choices about how we allocate it to activities that align with our priorities.

Now, turning our focus to leading teams, let's explore how leaders can harness the power of time for both personal enrichment and team development. Leveraging time means using it to its maximum advantage. Wise leaders ensure they do not neglect their own needs amidst their responsibilities. Overcommitting and neglecting self-care can lead to burnout and stress.

Prioritizing self-leadership is a key aspect of effectively leveraging time. Leaders who carve out dedicated blocks of time for self-renewal and relaxation are better equipped to lead from a place of inner peace, regardless of their leadership level.

Once leaders have taken care of their well-being, they can extend their time management skills to benefit their teams. One-on-one time with team members can be an invaluable investment, especially when they are facing challenges. As time is the "currency of life," dedicating time to mentor and guide team members can facilitate their growth and development.

By strategically leveraging their time, leaders not only enhance their own effectiveness but also contribute significantly to their team's success. In these moments, time becomes a powerful tool for transformation, benefiting the individual and the collective goals of the team. Since time is the "currency of life", you can invest some of it in a team member who otherwise might be seen as inadequate. Investing enough time into a person's development could be instrumental in helping the team member turn around and become a star performer. In this instance, time was leveraged in exchange for the good of the individual as well as the team.

A few steps to help leaders leverage time successfully:

1. Prioritize Self-Leadership:

- Effective leaders acknowledge that they can't lead effectively if they are physically, mentally, or emotionally drained. Therefore, leaders prioritize self-care activities such as exercise, meditation, hobbies, and spending quality time with loved ones.
- Disconnect from work-related stressors and engage in activities that bring them joy and relaxation.
- Establish clear boundaries between work and personal life. They avoid overcommitting and learn to say no when necessary to protect their personal time.

2. Identify Areas for Time Investment:

- Take time to assess the team's needs comprehensively. This involves not only evaluating the team's current performance but also identifying individual team members' strengths, weaknesses, and areas where they require support.

- Align time investment with the team's goals and objectives. For example, if the team is facing challenges in meeting deadlines, the leader might allocate extra time to provide guidance and resources to help the team overcome these obstacles.
- Effective leaders invest time in the team members' personal development. They identify high-potential individuals who would benefit from additional mentoring, training, or coaching to help them reach their full potential.

3. Strategically Allocate Time:

- Leaders create a plan that outlines how they will allocate their time to various tasks and responsibilities. This plan includes dedicated time blocks for team interactions, individual coaching sessions, and strategic planning.
- Leaders understand that unexpected challenges or opportunities may arise, requiring them to adjust their schedules accordingly. Being adaptable allows them to handle these situations effectively without feeling overwhelmed.
- Effective leaders also recognize that they can't do everything themselves. They delegate tasks and responsibilities to team members, empowering them to take ownership and contribute to the team's success. Delegation frees up the leader's time to focus on higher-priority activities that require their unique expertise.

By following these steps, leaders can leverage time not only for their personal well-being but also to maximize their impact on their teams. It's a holistic approach that ensures leaders are not only effective in their roles but also supportive of their team members' growth and development.

> *The miracle is not that we do this work, but that we are happy to do it.*
> -Mother Teresa

SUPERPOWER 10

Dirty Hands

The act of getting one's hands dirty is a well-known metaphor, signifying a commitment to contributing real value to a specific endeavor. Effective leaders are acutely aware of the advantages that come with rolling up their sleeves and immersing themselves in the work. The dirty hands superpower comes naturally to these leaders, driven by a profound understanding of the significance of leading by example. Gone are the days of merely issuing orders and deadlines; today's leaders recognize the importance of actively participating in achieving their objectives.

Effective leaders are acutely aware of the advantages that come with rolling up their sleeves.

Leaders who willingly get their hands dirty wield far greater influence over their team members than those who merely issue commands. Leadership success hinges on the ability to influence people, so it's essential for leaders to convey to their team members that they are ready and willing to dive in when needed.

10 Superpowers of Effective Leaders

Creating a toxic-free environment becomes nearly impossible when team members don't fully embrace their leader.

The most esteemed leaders often emerge from the ranks of their team members. They earn a higher level of respect because they can empathize with their teams, having experienced the same challenges and tasks. Leaders who shirk from getting their hands dirty when circumstances demand it only exacerbate toxicity, failing to add genuine value to the team.

I vividly recall an instance when I was organizing an event, and during the setup, it became apparent that several tables were missing. I approached the setup crew, who promptly informed me that they were following the event order precisely. In my effort to defuse the situation and ensure the best experience at the venue, I reached out to the senior manager, although he wasn't directly involved in our event's execution.

In an impressive display of leadership, he took off his jacket, despite the late hour, and retrieved tables from the storage area, setting them up in the room. His actions spoke volumes, leaving my client and me thoroughly impressed with his readiness to get his hands dirty.

Later, we had the opportunity to have lunch with this senior manager to discuss the event's challenges. I couldn't help but admire his commitment to making us feel heard. I told him that he was destined for a more significant and brighter future in his career. His leadership aspirations far exceeded his current position. Not long after our lunch meeting, I heard that he had not only been promoted but had also transferred to a more prestigious position at another property, accompanied by a substantial increase in pay.

Here are five steps a leader can take to embrace the practice of "getting their hands dirty" and leading by example:

1. Lead by Example:

- Effective leaders set the standard for their team by modeling the behavior they expect.
- Actively engage in the work alongside your team members. When they see you taking on tasks, it encourages them to do the same.

2. Stay Informed:

- Keep yourself well-informed about the day-to-day operations and challenges your team faces. This knowledge allows you to identify situations where your involvement or assistance might be required.

3. Be Accessible:

- Maintain an open line of communication with your team. Let them know that you are available to help when needed. Encourage team members to reach out to you when they require support or guidance.

4. Identify Critical Moments:

- Recognize key moments when your involvement can make a significant impact. These might include times of crisis, high workload, or when team members are facing challenges beyond their capacity.

5. Acknowledge Efforts:

- Don't forget to acknowledge and appreciate the hard work and dedication of your team members.
- Express gratitude for their contributions and, when possible, reward their efforts. This fosters a culture of teamwork and mutual respect.

By following these steps, leaders can effectively demonstrate their commitment to their team's success and create an environment where everyone is motivated to contribute their best efforts. For leaders, getting their hands dirty doesn't diminish their status or leadership position; instead, it fosters respect, honor, and loyalty among team members. It exemplifies a dedication to the team's success and reinforces the leader's commitment to leading by example.

Take a Moment

You made it! Tak a moment to make a list of action steps you will take to add value to your team.

_____

_____

_____

_____

_____

_____

_____

_____

_____

_____

Conclusion

In the journey of leadership, we find ourselves entrusted with a profound privilege—the privilege of guiding and nurturing a team towards success. Through the chapters of this book, we have explored the essential qualities and superpowers that effective leaders possess, each contributing to a harmonious and productive team environment.

As we conclude this exploration, it is crucial to emphasize that leadership is a privilege that carries the responsibility of adding value to our teams in every way possible. It is not merely a position of authority but a calling to cultivate an environment where individuals can flourish despite their differences.

By embracing the techniques and insights shared throughout this book, you are well-equipped to enhance your leadership ability. You can confidently define your leadership style, recognizing the uniqueness and potential of each team member. Armed with this knowledge, you are poised to create a culture that breathes life and vitality into the lives of your team members, both within and beyond the team setting. Leadership is not a passive role; it demands self-awareness and a willingness to assess our own contributions to the environments in which we work, live, and play. It requires active engagement, a commitment to listening, and a dedication to harnessing the power of silence, open-mindedness, and time management.

With these tools at your disposal, you have the potential to transform not only your own leadership journey but also the experiences of those you lead. You can neutralize toxic cultures, promote innovation, and empower your team members to reach their full potential.

In conclusion, the path to effective leadership is not static; it is a continuous journey of growth and self-improvement. As you reflect on the lessons and principles shared within these pages, my utmost desire is that your leadership journey proves to be not only beneficial but also deeply fulfilling. May you lead with purpose, inspire with empathy, and, above all, add lasting value to the lives of those you have the privilege to lead.

Thank you for embarking on this journey, and may your leadership shine brightly, creating a positive impact on your team, organization, and beyond.

About the Author

Natalie B. Green is not just an author; she is a beacon of inspiration, motivation, and empowerment. With a heart brimming with compassion and a deep-rooted desire to help individuals unearth their latent potential, she has dedicated her life to guiding people from diverse backgrounds toward discovering and embracing their God-given purpose. Natalie's journey as a prolific author, speaker, certified life coach, and personal mentor has touched the lives of countless individuals.

Natalie B. Green is the visionary behind two transformative women's fellowships, Unbroken Women's En-counter and Women of Purpose Fellowship and Conference. These platforms serve as catalysts for personal growth, empowerment, and spiritual enlightenment, drawing participants from all corners of life to embark on a journey of self-discovery and transformation.

In addition to her literary and mentoring pursuits, Natalie shares her wealth of knowledge and spiritual insight with her church congregation toward spiritual fulfillment and personal growth at Heart of God Ministries Church in Miami Gardens, FL, where her husband, James A. Green, Jr. is the Senior Pastor.

About the Author

Natalie B. Green's influence extends beyond her church and women's fellowships. She actively contributes to her community as a member of the Advisory Committee for the American Society for Public Administration (ASPA) South Florida, Elect Ladies Kingdom Network, and Created-N-Love Studios Foundation. Her commitment to community engagement underscores her dedication to making a meaningful impact on the lives of those around her.

As a speaker, Natalie is a force to be reckoned with—powerful, provocative, and energetic. Her wisdom is cultivated from over four decades of personal faith and trust in Jesus as Savior. She regularly shares her insights at corporate functions, workshops, empowerment conferences, and women's events, captivating audiences with her dynamic presence and profound message of personal transformation.

Behind her remarkable career and numerous achievements, Natalie remains devoted to her family. She treasures her role as a wife to her husband, James, a mother to her daughter, Melody and son-in-law, Gabriel, and a devoted Nana to Xavier. These personal connections have always been her greatest priority, fostering an atmosphere of love, support, and spiritual growth within her own home.

Natalie B. Green's life story is a testament to the power of faith, resilience, and unwavering dedication to the betterment of others. Through her books, including

Get Out of the Box: *Unleash the Giant in You* **and 10 Superpowers of Effective Leaders**: *Neutralizing Toxicity in Team Culture*, she continues to empower individuals to break free from self-imposed limitations and achieve their full potential. She remains steadfast in her mission to be a beacon of light and hope to those in need, leaving an indelible mark on the hearts and lives of those she touches.

GET OUT OF THAT BOX
Available everywhere books are sold!
www.nataliegreen.com

Daily Affirmations For The Superpowered Leader

1. My leadership is a privilege, and I use it to add value to the lives of others.
2. I am a master of active listening, understanding the needs and concerns of my team.
3. Silence is my superpower, allowing me to read the room and make impactful contributions.
4. I foster a culture of inclusivity, valuing the diversity and differences within my team.
5. Open-mindedness is my key to innovation and success as a leader.
6. I leverage time wisely, prioritizing self-care and investing in my team's growth.
7. I lead with empathy, acknowledging the emotions and perspectives of others.
8. Conflict is an opportunity for growth, and I handle it with grace and fairness.
9. I empower my team to achieve their full potential, unlocking their superpowers.
10. I continuously seek personal and professional growth to become a better leader.

I Am a Superpowered Leader!

Contact

Natalie B. Green
natalie@nataliebgreen.com
(305) 205-6820
www.nataliebgreen.com

www.facebook.com/NatalieGreenMinistries

www.instgram.com/Nataliebgreen

www.linkedin.com/in/natalie-b-green-1692b628a

Natalie B. Green
KEYNOTE SPEAKER, COACH, AUTHOR

If you and your team are looking for an experienced coach and speaker, Natalie is available to add value.

As a speaker, Natalie's goal is to inspire her audience and encourage them to think outside the box, empowering them to achieve their goals. **Topics include:**

- *The Superpowered Leader*
- *Fail to Forward*
- *Let's Go Up (Elevate)*
- *Blow Your Mind-Set*
- *D. I. G. Discover Inner Gold*

Natalie's job as a coach is to guide clients towards unlocking their true potential, and living a life full of purpose and significance.

- *Life & Business*
- *Mindset Shifts*
- *Personal Growth*
- *Spiritual Development*

www.ingramcontent.com/pod-product-compliance
Lightning Source LLC
Chambersburg PA
CBHW070528010526
44110CB00050B/2271